If I REALLY WANTED TO

BEAT STRESS

I WOULD . . .

RACINE, WI

If I Really Wanted to Beat Stress, I Would . . .
ISBN: 978-1-970103-98-4 - *Paperback*
ISBN: 978-1-970103-99-1 - *Hardcover*
ISBN: 978-1-970103-51-9 - *Ebook*
Copyright © 2022 by Honor Books
Racine, WI

INTRODUCTION

A little stress is a good thing. It keeps us on our toes and busy pursuing our dreams. However, our bodies were never designed to handle the formidable amount of stress we face in today's complicated world. Unless we deal with it wisely, it will rob us of our health and our happiness.

The simple insights contained in this small book can't guarantee that your life will be stress-free— nothing can. They can suggest ways to deal positively with stress and mitigate its destructive effects. So join us as we learn to tune out stress. Who knows, you may be tuning in to a whole new frequency of peace and happiness at the same time.

GOD BLESS YOU IN YOUR QUEST!

If I really wanted to Beat stress, I would . . .

Prepare for It

"DISTRESS" IS MOST OFTEN STRESS THAT HASN'T BEEN ADDRESSED.

Stress happens. Daily. To everyone . . . including you. Along with good, old everyday traffic jams and annoying telemarketers, your life will sometimes hit more than just a bump in the road. You may be dealing with unemployment, divorce, illness, a new baby, or a death in the family. And your body knows it.

The best way to deal with stress is to beat it before it begins to beat you. Develop healthy habits in diet, sleep, and exercise. Invest the time it takes to build healthy relationships. Recognize God's sovereignty over your life. When an unexpected crisis catches you off guard, give yourself a break. Cut out the nonessentials, and take the time you need to get your feet back on solid ground.

God will help you deal with whatever hard things come up when the time comes.

MATTHEW 6:34 MSG

If I really wanted to Beat stress, I would . . .

Pinpoint my "Stressors"

WHAT YOU CAN'T SEE CAN HURT YOU.

S tress has earned a bad reputation. It's really a God-given response that triggers your body for fight or flight. It can spur you into action, saving your life in an emergency. But when feelings of stress linger or are triggered for little or no reason at all, they can deplete your body's resources. They can make you susceptible to heart disease, high blood pressure, even the common cold. You can become forgetful, disorganized, and less creative. Prolonged feelings of stress can also result in anxiety, aggression, or depression.

What are your biggest "stressors"? Procrastination? Perfectionism? Disorganization? A dead-end job? Illness? Unresolved conflict? Finances? Recognizing your main sources of stress is the first step toward reducing their effect on you.

Know thyself.

PLUTARCH

IF I REALLY WANTED TO
BEAT STRESS, I WOULD . . .

STOP PLAYING THE LONE RANGER

CONTINUALLY FLYING SOLO CAN TAKE YOU SO LOW!

The Lone Ranger didn't defeat the bad guys all alone. He had the help of his faithful friend, Tonto, not to mention his lightning-fast horse, Silver. Human beings just aren't designed to conquer life on their own. Whether it's moving furniture or battling depression, some situations require a call for help.

Of course, you may be one of those people who has trouble asking for help. If so, just remember that the help you need is available, regardless of whether it's physical, emotional, financial, or spiritual. It may take a little research and vulnerability to connect with the right counselor, friend, or family member, but sending up an SOS when you need it, is a sure sign of maturity—not weakness.

Sticks in a bundle are unbreakable.

KENYAN PROVERB

IF I REALLY WANTED TO
BEAT STRESS, I WOULD . . .

RECOGNIZE THAT IMAGE ISN'T EVERYTHING

A MAN IS MEASURED BY THE SIZE OF HIS HEART, NOT HIS HOME.

How much time and energy do you put into portraying a certain image to those around you? Does it affect the way you dress, the car you buy, the neighborhood you live in, the jokes you laugh at, or even the people you choose to be seen with? Trying to be someone you're not is a source of stress that only grows with time.

Playing charades may be fun at a party, but in real life it leaves you feeling that the real you just isn't good enough. Take some time to evaluate whom you are creating yourself in the image of and why. Is the bottom line really worth it?

God created man in his own image.

GENESIS 1:27

IF I REALLY WANTED TO
BEAT STRESS, I WOULD . . .

TIPTOE
THROUGH THE
TULIPS

When life is anything but "a walk in the park," that's the best time to take one.

There's something both miraculous and soothing about being around living, growing things that don't talk back. Working in your garden or taking a walk in the park is a natural stress reliever. Breathe in the fragrance of freshly turned earth. Watch trees dance in the wind. Look for hidden wildflowers.

Even out of season, when the trees are bare and the grass has turned to straw, you'll be amazed at the life you'll find hiding in the most unexpected places. All it takes is slowing down long enough to look. When Jesus faced the most stressful event of His life here on earth, He went to a garden to pray. Why not follow His example today?

Were there no God we would he in this glorious world with grateful hearts; and no one to thank.

Christina Rossetti

If I really wanted to Beat stress, I would . . .

Put it Back Where I Found It

ORGANIZATION ALLOWS RELAXATION.

The tape dispenser is missing in action. The cell phone is ringing but not long enough to reveal its hiding place. You have to run a quick errand, but the car keys have disappeared. Your new camera goes on the fritz and the warranty is, well . . . you're sure you didn't throw it away!

How much time do you waste looking for something that should be right under your nose? How much extra stress is added to your day because you can't find what you need when you need it? Searching for lost items can be overwhelmingly stressful. Your mother was right: "A place for everything and everything in its place" is a simple solution to a common problem.

The more possessions, the more worry.

HILLEL

If I really wanted to beat stress, I would . . .

Let Go of the Past

A REARVIEW MIRROR IS FOR BACKING UP, NOT MOVING FORWARD.

No amount of energy can change the past. But holding on to yesterday can rob you of energy you need to handle today. Try to see the upside of past mistakes or misfortune by treating them as colorful material for your life story—motivators that helped you move in new directions.

Of course, there may be some areas of pain and regret that you won't be able to deal with alone. In that case, talk to a counselor or close friend. And don't hesitate to ask for God's help. He's a great listener. Just opening up about what's holding you back can help you put the past where it belongs—in the past.

Forget the former things; do not dwell on the past. See, I am doing a new thing!

ISAIAH 43:18-19

If I really wanted to Beat stress, I would . . .

EXERCISE

Be wise! Exercise!

I t's no secret that exercise is a great antidote for stress. But "just doing it," is often difficult. When you're stressed, your first inclination is to don your pajamas and head for the couch—not the gym. So is it really such a big deal?

When it comes to your body, exercise and stress are polar opposites. Regular exercise helps you build a type of "immunity" to the ill effects of stress and handle more with less burnout. But as in all things, moderation is the key. Overdoing it to the point of pain or fatigue diminishes its benefits. Walk, run, bike, or bend, but whatever you do, get moving!

An early morning walk is a blessing for the whole day.

Henry David Thoreau

If I really wanted to Beat stress, I would . . .

Cut The Caffeine

WHEN YOU'RE ON THE GO, SAY "NO" TO THAT CUP OF JOE!

Can't face the day until you're fully caffeinated? You're not alone. Whether it's coffee, tea, or soda, caffeine does give you an instant boost . . . then, drops you like a ton of bricks.

When facing an already stressful situation, drinking two to three cups of coffee can double your body's production of cortisol, a stress hormone. Soon you're feeling jittery and anxious, rather than energized and alert. Kicking the caffeine habit can help reduce your anxiety level. But if the mere thought makes you break out in a cold sweat, why not compromise? Counter each glass of caffeine with the same amount of water. It's a healthy habit that will help you cut back on caffeine while keeping you hydrated.

The only way to keep your health is to eat what you don't want, drink what you don't like, and do what you'd druther not.

MARK TWAIN

IF I REALLY WANTED TO
BEAT STRESS, I WOULD . . .

REFUSE TO LIVE
IN THE FUTURE

THE PRESENT TIME IS THE TIME TO BE PRESENT.

Are you stressed-out today by worrying about what's coming tomorrow? Maybe it's a dental appointment or an important presentation at work. Maybe it's anticipating a doctor's call over the results of a medical test. Maybe it's the fear of retirement or the end of a relationship.

Today's stress could even be about something positive, like preparing for vacation, a possible promotion, working long hours now for a payoff later. But your body was only designed to handle one day at a time. Worrying acts like a magnifying glass—everything starts to look bigger than it really is. Putting tomorrow in God's hands and doing what you can today is the best way to wipe out worry.

Do not worry about tomorrow, for tomorrow will worry about itself. Each day has enough trouble of its own.

MATTHEW 6:34

If I really wanted to Beat stress, I would . . .

Tie up Loose Ends

YOU CAN HANG YOURSELF WITH LOOSE ENDS.

Watch stopped? Vase chipped? Vacuum making sounds that can only be described as a captive rodent's cries for help? Don't set it aside hoping it will miraculously fix itself. Put it in the "fix-it" box. (Larger items, such as cars that need tuning, will be better off relegated to a corresponding "fix-it" list!)

Give yourself one week to deal with what's in the box. Schedule larger jobs as weekend projects. But a minor repair or calling a professional for an appointment takes just a few minutes. Do it right away. Putting it off gives it the power to intimidate you. And one more thing, if the item is too far gone, don't put it off-budget for a replacement.

Nothing valuable can be lost by taking time.

ABRAHAM LINCOLN

IF I REALLY WANTED TO
BEAT STRESS, I WOULD . . .

BREAK MY DAY DOWN INTO BITE-SIZED PIECES

A MOUNTAIN IS CLIMBED ONE PEAK AT A TIME.

One look at today's schedule and you're ready to climb back into bed—forget the big picture. But the day will seem more manageable if you take it one moment at a time. Think about a jigsaw puzzle. When you dump a thousand pieces on the table, it looks like a mess, an overwhelming impossibility. But you start by finding the edge pieces, looking for corners, sorting by color, and slowly the final picture begins to take shape.

If today looks like a five-thousand-piece puzzle, start small. Break down big projects into smaller jobs. Handle only this morning or this hour or the next five minutes. Your day may turn out to be an unexpected masterpiece.

A mountain is climbed one step at a time.

PERUVIAN PROVERB

IF I REALLY WANTED TO
BEAT STRESS, I WOULD . . .

BREATHE IN,
BREATHE OUT

BREATHE EASIER BY BREATHING DEEPER.

Shallow breathing makes you feel tired. It lowers levels of oxygen and raises levels of carbon monoxide in your blood. It can also make your heart rate and blood pressure rise—an added stress on your body.

When you feel tension mounting, try this deep-breathing exercise. Put your feet flat on the floor and rest your hands in your lap. Begin to relax your body by dropping your shoulders and closing your eyes. Then take a deep breath through your nose, while slowly counting to four. Exhale through your mouth to a slow count of four. Do this four times. You should feel your body relaxing and your fatigue lifting.

The Lord God formed the man from the dust of the ground and breathed into his nostrils the breath of life, and the man became a living being.

GENESIS 2:7

IF I REALLY WANTED TO BEAT STRESS, I WOULD . . .

SING IN THE CAR

EVEN IF YOU CAN'T CARRY A TUNE, A TUNE CAN HELP CARRY YOU.

Caught in rush hour? Drowning in the deep end of the car pool? Running the same old errands week after week? Instead of taking out your frustrations by telling others how to drive, give your vocal chords a harmonious workout. Turn on your favorite radio station. Put in a tape or CD that really gets your blood pumping. Then sing along. Croon. Warble. Worship. Hum. Use your steering wheel as a drum set.

And don't worry about what other drivers may think. You'll probably make them smile. Before you know it, you'll have arrived at your destination with a smile of your own.

Music hath charms to soothe the savage beast.

WILLIAM CONGREVE

IF I REALLY WANTED TO
BEAT STRESS, I WOULD . . .

WEAR THE SIZE
THAT FITS

BEAUTY IS MEASURED IN SMILES, NOT POUNDS.

In the fashion- and weight-conscious world we live in, deciding what to wear can be a red- hot source of stress. "Will I look good?" often outweighs, "Will I feel good?" And if some of your favorite outfits happen to be fitting a bit snug, you can find yourself tugging, pulling, and readjusting throughout the day.

People change—so do their sizes. Just because you wore one size in high school doesn't mean it's yours for the rest of your life. If you need to lose a few pounds, watch your diet and remember to exercise. In the meantime, give yourself room to breathe. No one knows your size but you.

I pray thee O God, that I may be beautiful within.

SOCRATES

If I really wanted to beat stress, I would . . .

Count my Blessings

A THANKFUL HEART IS A HAPPY HEART.

A child living in a Third World country wrote a letter to his American sponsor describing how his home had been flooded by recent storms. "The good news," he wrote, "is at least now, we have fish!" There is good to be found in even the most stressful situations. Taking time to not only notice your blessings but also to savor them helps you keep things in perspective.

What are you thankful for today? Why not take some time each morning to consider that question. Then take your answer to God with a heart full of gratitude and praise. What better way could there be to begin your day?

From the fullness of his grace we have all received one blessing after another.

JOHN 1:16

HOP INTO THE TUB

Rubber Duckies Have It Lucky!

Hydrotherapy—it's a fancy name for a nice, warm bath. But whatever you call it, a trip to the tub is a time-tested stress reliever. It calms the lungs, heart, stomach, and endocrine system, while relieving tension from sore muscles. Where else on earth can you find freedom from gravity?

To get the most out of your tub time, don't make it too hot. The least stressful temperature is when your body doesn't feel the temperature at all. Bubble bath can dry your skin, so try some aromatic oils like mint or lavender. Then lower the lights and just relax. Scheduling your bath before bedtime will also help you fall asleep more easily and sleep more deeply.

True joy is serene.

Seneca

If I really wanted to Beat stress, I would . . .

PET A PET

GOD'S CREATURES ARE A REFLECTION OF HIS LOVE.

When life seems overwhelming, snuggle with your Siamese, bond with your beagle, gape at your guppies, pontificate with your parakeet—spending time with any pet will do.

Since the late eighteenth century, physicians have acknowledged the health- related benefits of caring for a pet. Pets can reduce feelings of loneliness, isolation, and depression. The act of petting them can lower your blood pressure and relieve muscle tension. Best of all, pets can help you reconnect emotionally. Even if you're not a "hugger," a pet can give you the opportunity to express deep emotions in a physical way without the fear of rejection. Pets can be a bonanza of unconditional love and acceptance.

Until one has loved an animal, part of one's soul remains unawakened.

ANATOLE FRANCE

IF I REALLY WANTED TO
BEAT STRESS, I WOULD . . .

SLEEP LIKE A BABY

Proper rest fights stress.

As a baby, you craved a consistent bedtime, demanding the proper amount of sleep by wailing until you got it. But then you grew up. Adults often fight those same healthy urges and live lives on the edge of exhaustion.

Tonight, try babying yourself. Dim the lights for the last few hours before bedtime. Drink a little warm milk. Be a creature of habit, keeping your bedtime and rising time consistent. If you need a bit more sleep on occasion, go to bed twenty to thirty minutes earlier. Sleeping in during the morning leaves you with a jet-lagged feeling—without the benefit of arriving at a vacation destination.

You've kept track of my every toss and turn
through the sleepless nights.

PSALM 56:8 MSG

If I really wanted to Beat stress, I would . . .

Delegate, Delegate, Delegate

THERE'S NO "I" IN "TEAMWORK."

It feels good to accomplish something on your own—to receive accolades for doing the impossible, to be the one responsible for a noteworthy success. But life is a team sport.

Delegation isn't always easy. People won't often do things exactly the way you want them to. Sometimes, they even let you down. But more often than not, they add something to a project that you never could— their own unique talents, ideas, and twist on life. So whether you're a businessman who likes to go solo with your paperwork or a mother who feels it's easier to do the dishes yourself than enlist your kids' help, give yourself a break and delegate.

If I have been able to see farther than others, it is because I have stood on the shoulders of giants.

SIR ISAAC NEWTON

IF I REALLY WANTED TO
BEAT STRESS, I WOULD . . .

GO FOR THE
H₂O

TAP OR "GOURMET," MAKE WATER YOUR BEVERAGE OF CHOICE.

Are you experiencing a lack of energy in the middle of a busy day? Often a drop in energy is a sign that you're dehydrated. By the time you're feeling thirsty, you've already lost 2 to 3 percent of your body fluid. This lowers your blood volume, making your heart pump harder to get blood to your brain.

Give yourself an energy boost with a cold glass of water. Any chilled beverage is a wake-up call for your body, but water is what your body really craves. Try to include at least eight glasses in your daily diet. Add more soups and fresh fruits and vegetables, and you'll have more natural energy to draw on when you face stressful situations.

Water is good; it benefits all things.

LAO-TZU

If I Really Wanted to Beat Stress, I Would . . .

Take Off My Watch

UNDERSTANDING WHAT MAKES YOU "TICK" IS SOMETHING TO "TOCK" ABOUT.

I n a rush? Clock watching can actually waste time and increase your anxiety. This weekend, try observing your inner clock rather than the watch on your wrist. Eat when you're hungry. Sleep when you're tired. Work or play when you're energized. Then, take what you've learned about your own daily rhythms and apply it to your regular schedule. It can help you get more done in less time.

Use the time of day when you're most alert to plan, organize, and tackle your toughest projects. If you fall into an afternoon slump, schedule tasks that don't take a lot of brain power, like returning phone calls. And when your body says, "Time for bed," listen!

Hour by hour, I place my days in your hand.

PSALM 31:15 MSG

If I really wanted to Beat stress, I would . . .

Cultivate Quiet

A LITTLE PEACE AND QUIET HELPS YOU KEEP PACE RATHER THAN QUIT.

Horns honking. Kids screaming. Phones ringing. Radios blaring. Noise is a constant stressor. It can increase your pulse rate and blood pressure, make your adrenaline surge, and deplete your energy. Your body works harder to complete tasks when it is trying to tune out noise at the same time. So give it a little help.

During the day, take a break from background music or television. Purchase an electric fan to muffle the sounds that distract you while working or falling asleep. Buy a pair of earplugs to help you sleep at night or take a "quiet break" during the day.

How rare to find a soul still enough to hear God speak.

FRANCOIS DE FENELON

IF I REALLY WANTED TO
BEAT STRESS, I WOULD . . .

DO WHATEVER I'VE BEEN PUTTING OFF

"TOMORROW" IS OFTEN THE BUSIEST DAY OF THE WEEK.

What's at the bottom of your "to do" list? Or is it at the top, day after day after day? Let's face it, some things are just not fun. Cleaning the bathroom. Getting a root canal. Confronting someone about an ongoing problem. Unfortunately, the longer you put off unpleasant tasks, the more unpleasant they become— and the more stress they add to your life.

All procrastination really does is delay the inevitable. Though your mind may be saying, "Phew! I can relax because I don't have to do that," your body is whispering, "But I know I'm gonna have to make time for it soon!" Today, why not take one task you've been putting off and "just do it!" You'll be glad you did.

Never do today what you can put off till tomorrow.

MATTHEW BROWNE

IF I REALLY WANTED TO BEAT STRESS, I WOULD . . .

JUST SAY "NO!"

ALWAYS SAYING "YES" IS A SURE CAUSE OF STRESS.

Does your mouth ever say "yes" while your heart is screaming "no"? Being assertive is sometimes viewed as being insensitive, unkind, or self-serving. But it's really just being honest and fair. Your time and your needs are as important as anyone else's.

This doesn't mean that your "boundaries" should keep you from ever going out of your way for someone else. It just means you don't let anger and frustration build by trying to live up to a "yes" that never should have been said. Procrastination, forgetfulness, doing a halfhearted job, or quitting at the last moment are often just backhanded ways of saying "no." So be considerate and just say "no" in the first place.

Let your "Yes" be yes, and your "No," no.

JAMES 5:12

IF I REALLY WANTED TO
BEAT STRESS, I WOULD . . .

BUILD SLACK INTO MY SCHEDULE

ONE WHO HURRIES OFTEN STUMBLES ALONG THE WAY.

L iving life to the limit has its drawbacks. It often leads to over scheduling, trying to cram twenty-four hours worth of activity into a day that hopefully includes only sixteen waking hours.

Hurrying can be as serious a stressor as worrying. Just looking at a list of too much to do and too little time to do it can get the adrenaline flowing. So why not cut yourself some slack? Schedule only 75 percent of your waking hours, instead of 110 percent. And don't forget to build in time for the unexpected traffic jam or call from an old friend. Cutting yourself some slack can prevent a lot of stress.

This perpetual hurry of business and company ruins me in soul if not in body.

WILLIAM WILBERFORCE

If I really wanted to beat stress, I would . . .

Obey the Traffic Laws

CRIME DOESN'T PAY.

A flashing red light in your rearview mirror can set your body on overload and your already-crazy schedule into a tailspin. Speeding, running yellow lights, and rolling through stop signs are not reliable time savers. And the toll they could take on your life could be more costly than a ticket.

Breaking traffic laws puts your body on alert, constantly on guard for an approaching police car. Why not give yourself a few extra minutes for every commute, car pool, and errand? Learn to build it into your schedule. If you arrive early you'll even have time to catch your breath, something your body could use.

Every action of our lives touches on some
chord that will vibrate in eternity.

EDWIN HUBBEL CHAPIN

IF I REALLY WANTED TO
BEAT STRESS, I WOULD . . .

REFUSE TO COMPARE MYSELF TO OTHERS

WHY BE A COPY WHEN YOU CAN BE AN ORIGINAL?

It's been said, "When God made you, He broke the mold." And though the expression is usually meant to be humorous, it's true! Since the beginning of time, and until its end, there will be only one you. That means comparing yourself to others makes very little sense.

If you want to make a worthwhile comparison, try comparing yourself to yourself. Are you growing in positive ways? Using your talents to the best of your ability? Becoming someone you could look up to? Use your impulse to make comparisons as a self-improvement exercise. Why stress out trying to imitate someone you were never created to be?

Each of us is an original.

GALATIANS 5:26 MSG

IF I REALLY WANTED TO BEAT STRESS, I WOULD . . .

TWIST AND SHOUT!

THERE'S GREAT BENEFIT IN A LITTLE BOOGIE-WOOGIE.

Kids dance to any music that moves them, unlike adults who often have to be dragged out onto a dance floor. Adults can be so self-conscious about how they look, they forget how great dancing feels. Dancing feels good for a reason. It stimulates endorphins, your body's natural mood-lifting hormones. It's also great exercise that has the added benefit of helping you express your feelings. That's a great combination of stress relievers.

So why be a wallflower? Take a dance class or just turn up the stereo and move, with or without a partner. Who knew relieving stress could be so much fun?

When you finally allow yourself to trust joy and embrace it, you will find you dance with everything.

EMMANUEL

If I really wanted to Beat stress, I would . . .

Call a Friend

A TRUE FRIEND ONLY GETS IN YOUR WAY WHEN YOU'RE GOING IN THE WRONG DIRECTION.

Having a heart-to-heart talk with a good friend gives you a chance to vent all of the frustrations, disappointments, and pent-up emotions you've been carrying around on your stressed-out shoulders. Explaining your problems to someone else helps you sort out the trivial from the traumatic. Discussing stressors in your life also helps you organize and categorize them in your own mind, leading you closer to a possible resolution.

Hearing someone else say, "That must be tough," is a good reminder that you don't have to feel guilty about being stressed when life is difficult. And it gives you the reassurance that whatever you're facing, you don't have to face it alone.

Friends are needed both for joy and sorrow.

JEWISH PROVERB

If I really wanted to beat stress, I would . . .

Use It or Lose It

Stop Clutter Before it Starts.

Taking care of "stuff" takes energy. So why expend your much-needed energy on something you don't really need? If you haven't worn it, played with it, cooked with it, or looked at it for more than a year, why not donate it to someone who might actually need it?

The less you have to organize, the easier and less stressful it is. A good spring cleaning could also benefit you with a little extra cash from a garage sale or a tax deduction from donations to a charitable organization. So before you purchase something new, ask yourself, "Do I really need this, or will it end up in the 'give away' pile next year?"

A time to search and a time to give up, a time to keep and a time to throw away.

Ecclesiastes 3:6

If I really wanted to beat stress, I would . . .

Act like a kid

When You're on the Run, Make Some Time for Fun.

Do you ever long for the days when your only job was to go outside and play? If not, perhaps you've forgotten the simple joys of having fun. In adulthood, "play" is often synonymous with competition. If winning matters more than playing, your "playtimes" will do little to help relieve stress, other than provide a momentary diversion and a bit of physical exercise.

How long has it been since you exercised your imagination? If you can't recall, it's probably out of shape. Exercising your creativity by painting a picture, writing a poem, even daydreaming about the shape of clouds in a summer sky are natural stress relievers. And it's downright fun. Just ask a kid.

You can discover more about a person in an hour of play than in a year of conversation.

PLATO

IF I REALLY WANTED TO BEAT STRESS, I WOULD . . .

FAIL

EVERY FAILURE HOLDS THE SEED
OF SUCCESS.

To fail seems almost un-American. Well, except for the fact that Christopher Columbus' failure to find Asia actually led him to discover America. Failure happens. Even Pepsi-Cola went bankrupt three times before finding it's current success. It was even offered for sale to the Coca-Cola Company. Coca-Cola passed.

Just because you've failed doesn't make you a failure. It just makes you human. Fear of failure will not only put your body under additional stress but limit your chances for success in the future. You can't succeed without taking risks. There is something to be learned from every endeavor, whether you regard it as a triumph or a turkey.

The glory is not in never failing, but in rising every time you fall.

CHINESE PROVERB

IF I REALLY WANTED TO
BEAT STRESS, I WOULD . . .

FORGIVE OTHERS

FORGIVING OTHERS IS A GIFT TO YOURSELF.

People hurt other people—intentionally or not, it's a fact of life. Holding on to that hurt forces you to carry a load that your body, particularly your heart, was not designed to handle.

Forgiveness is a gift—no strings attached. Forgiving others, regardless of whether or not they're repentant or have any remorse, isn't something to be taken lightly. It doesn't mean validating the action or excusing the offender. It means fully understanding how much you were hurt and choosing to release the offending person in spite of it. It's something you can only do fully through God, because He has done it so freely for you.

Be gentle and ready to forgive; never hold grudges. Remember, the Lord forgave you, so you must forgive others.

COLOSSIANS 3:13 TLB

IF I REALLY WANTED TO BEAT STRESS, I WOULD . . .

LEARN TO PAUSE AND REFLECT

SLOW DOWN BEFORE YOU HIT SOMETHING.

The faster the speed, the harder it is to bring a car to a complete stop. The same goes for life. When you're going 150 miles an hour to meet a self-imposed schedule, it takes discipline to slow down, let alone stop. The only thing that puts on the brakes seems to be the unexpected. A flood or a trip to the emergency room frees up that "must do" list in no time.

Why wait for catastrophe? Just taking a moment to evaluate what you're doing and why helps put life back into perspective. If you never take time to stop and consider where you're headed, you may discover you've arrived at a destination you never intended to reach.

Beware when the great God lets loose a thinker on this planet.

RALPH WALDO EMERSON

If I really wanted to Beat stress, I would . . .

Eat even Fast Food Slowly

DON'T LET STRESS DICTATE YOUR GROCERY LIST.

Are you living hand-to-mouth? In other words, when you're stressed, do you automatically reach for something to eat? The worst foods to consume while under stress are chocolate, coffee, ice cream, and alcohol. But it doesn't take much research to know that these are some of the foods people reach for to alleviate stress, at least emotionally.

Letting emotions drive your eating habits has an adverse effect on how stressed you feel, but it also takes the joy out of eating. So, when you're going to eat—eat without doing anything else. Taste your food. Chew it slowly. If you reach for a cookie, savor it. Enjoying one fully is more satisfying than downing five without noticing.

That everyone may eat and drink, and find satisfaction in all his toil—this is the gift of God.

ECCLESIASTES 3:13

If I really wanted to Beat stress, I would . . .

Short-Circuit Time Stealers

YOU CAN'T KILL TIME WITHOUT HURTING YOURSELF.

W here does the time go? To get a clue, keep a log of your activities for a few days. Fifteen minute increments is picky enough. How much time do you spend each day surfing the Internet? Reading the paper? Chatting on the phone? Running to the grocery store for one or two items? Watching TV shows you don't even care about?

Review your log, then decide which "time stealers" you want to cut down on or eliminate. Screen unwanted calls with caller ID. Only check e-mail once a day. Don't open junk mail—toss it. Group errands to save time in the car. See how much time you can recover in your day. Then spend it doing what you enjoy most.

The time we have at our disposal every day is elastic.

MARCEL PROUST

If I really wanted to Beat stress, I would . . .

Save for a Rainy Day

EARNING MONEY IS EASIER THAN KEEPING IT.

Debt is a four-letter word. It puts not only a strain on your budget, your marriage, and your future but extra stress on your body. And much of the time, credit purchases are born out of emotion more than necessity. Buying something feels good, momentarily. But how does your body react, not to mention your spouse, when you open the credit card statement? The thrill is gone.

Living within your means takes self-denial and delayed gratification, not popular terms in today's society. But saving to make a purchase and putting aside ten percent of your income for life's unexpected little catastrophes is not only wise, it's also good for your health.

A man is rich in proportion to the number of things he can do without. Beware of all enterprises that require new clothes.

HENRY DAVID THOREAU

If I really wanted to beat stress, I would . . .

Saunter in The Sun

WHEN YOU'RE ON THE RUN, FIND A PLACE IN THE SUN.

Looking for a natural boost of caffeine? Try spending ten minutes in the sun. In a recent study, researchers at the University of Massachusetts found depression, hostility, anger, and anxiety to be highest during the winter and lowest in the summer. Exposure to natural light, or the lack thereof, can play a part in your moods.

So when stress and anxiety set in, take a walk. Being outside, even on a cloudy day, is an instant stress reliever. If it isn't possible to get outside, spend a few minutes sitting near a sunny window. If your body doesn't get enough natural light, it goes into a sleep mode—enough to stress out anyone with a full "to do" list.

I stroll at leisure with God in the sunlit fields of life.

PSALM 56:13 MSG

If I Really Wanted to Beat Stress, I Would . . .

Reread Words of Encouragement

WHY NOT ADD TO SOMEONE ELSE'S "ATTA BOY" FILE TODAY?

There's a certain allure about being "home on the range." Watching the deer and the antelope play sounds moderately entertaining, but the real draw is being where "seldom was heard a discouraging word." These days, words of criticism and discouragement seem to be everywhere.

That's where an "atta boy" file comes in handy. Saving and rereading notes from friends, birthday and thank-you cards, letters of recognition from work, etc. can help encourage a heavy heart. If your file is still in the embryonic stages, there are other letters filled with words of encouragement found in the Bible. Along with the Epistles, reading the Gospels and the Psalms can lift your spirit and help alleviate your feelings of stress.

One kind word can warm three winter months.

JAPANESE PROVERB

If I really wanted to beat stress, I would . . .

Take up a Hobby

TO LOVE A HOBBY, YOU'VE GOT TO SPEND TIME WITH IT.

If you were given a day of free time to spend doing what you love, what would you do? Canoe? Play guitar? Paint? Fish? Quilt? Hobbies are as varied as the people who love them. If you can't think of one thing outside of work, television, or just hanging out that you really have a passion for, it's time to discover a hobby you can love.

A hobby that's a perfect fit will involve a combination of anti-stressors, like utilizing your natural abilities, learning to master a skill or challenge, and absorbing your mind in something other than your daily problems. Hobbies can give you a sense of control and achievement. Best of all, they're just plain fun.

Happiness is everywhere, and its spring is in our own heart.

JOHN RUSKIN

If I really wanted to Beat stress, I would . . .

Forgive Myself

A GUILT TRIP IS NO VACATION.

Guilt is a heavy load to carry, not only emotionally but also physically. It may be well earned or just a lifelong accumulation of "should haves." Whatever the source, it's an invisible stressor that won't lose its grip on you until you give up your hold on it.

Begin by determining where your guilt comes from. Is what you're hearing the truth? Is there something you should do, fess up to, make up for? If so, take care of it. If your guilt is based on unfounded words of condemnation placed on you by someone in your past, then relief will come only when you recognize and discard them. God's already promised His forgiveness. What's holding you back from forgiving yourself?

Let us draw near to God . . . in full assurance
of faith, having our hearts sprinkled to cleanse
us from a guilty conscience.

HEBREWS 10:22

If I really wanted to beat stress, I would . . .

Read a Good Book

THE ONLY VALUABLE BOOK IS AN OPEN BOOK.

"Once upon a time" really can be magical words. They can calm you down after a busy day and help you prepare for a good night's sleep. Unfortunately, most people are more apt to reach for the remote than a good book.

If you are one of those, remember that reading has more relaxation benefits than watching television. It gives you control. You choose the pace, the time, the place. It's portable, ready at a moment's notice, and it gives your imagination a needed workout. The selection of material is almost endless. So pick up anything from a comic book to Shakespeare and lose yourself for a while. But if you're serious about relaxing, leave the work-related books at the office.

Reading is to the mind what exercise is to the body.

JOSEPH ADDISON

IF I REALLY WANTED TO BEAT STRESS, I WOULD . . .

HIRE A MAID OR LOWER YOUR STANDARDS

OWN YOUR HOME, BUT DON'T LET YOUR HOME OWN YOU.

Unless you're Martha Stewart, living gets messy, especially if you add a kid or two, pets, appliances that break down, and an occasional bout with the flu. Keeping a house that looks "magazine perfect" is a full-time job and doesn't allow much time for real living.

The flip side is that utter chaos can be a stressor and time stealer as well. So what chores have to be done? Clean clothes, washed dishes, and groceries void of mold are all important. But dusting your baseboards? Family delegation and an occasional all-out spring cleaning, mixed with simply putting things away after you use them, is enough to keep most houses up and running, as well as more relaxed and inviting.

Where there is room in the heart there is always room in the house.

THOMAS MOORE

IF I REALLY WANTED TO
BEAT STRESS, I WOULD . . .

DO NOTHING,
THEN REST
AFTERWARDS

TAKE TIME TO UNWIND FROM THE DAILY GRIND.

How long has it been since you took a vacation? Not a few days tacked onto a business trip. Not a whirlwind tour of twelve countries in six days. Not time off from work to catch up on projects around the house. A real vacation means relaxation.

Everyone needs a little downtime. Whether it's a long weekend or the luxury of a week or two, forsake deadlines. Read. Walk. Become deeply engrossed in conversations about life, love, faith—anything but work—with someone you care about. If sitting in one place for too long drives you nuts, go for a bike ride, play tennis, swim. Just don't turn your vacation into another "got to do" list.

He makes me lie down in green pastures, he leads me beside quiet waters, he restores my soul.

PSALM 23:2-3

If I really wanted to Beat stress, I would . . .

Take Mini-Vacations Every Day

IT ONLY TAKES A MINUTE TO SAVOR THE MOMENT.

One or two weeks of vacation a year isn't enough to combat 350 days of stressed-out living. So why not take a mini-vacation today? It doesn't have to involve the hassle of luggage and plane tickets. You can do it right where you are. All it takes is a little attitude adjustment.

Lunch with a friend, a walk around the block, even watching clouds roll by your office window are all excellent ways to relax your harried heart. Just focus on the simple pleasure of the moment. Don't let familiarity with your surroundings blind you to the miracles hidden in every ordinary day. It's a vacation you can't afford not to take.

The real voyage of discovery consists not in seeking new landscapes, but in having new eyes.

MARCEL PROUST

If I really wanted to beat stress, I would . . .

Get Down and Dirty

FORGET HOW YOU LOOK AND HAVE FUN!

Remember what it was like as a kid to go out and play? To jump in mud puddles? Dig to China? Hike through the "wilderness"? All without caring what your clothes looked like when you got home?

Adulthood is so careful—and clean! Forgetting about your appearance and heading out to hike, bike, raft, play sports, or even plant a garden is not only therapeutic but also a lot of fun. When you're totally involved in an activity, you're less conscious of your own insecurities and problems. And the exercise you get will benefit your mood. The only downside may be an extra load of laundry, but at least you'll do it with a smile.

A man wrapped up in himself makes a very small bundle.

BENJAMIN FRANKLIN

IF I REALLY WANTED TO
BEAT STRESS, I WOULD . . .

TREAT MYSELF TO A MASSAGE

MASSAGE IS GOOD FOR THE BODY AND SOUL.

A massage not only feels good, it's good for you. The motions used in massage trigger a natural relaxation response in your body, which slows down the whole nervous system. It also increases circulation, which helps relieve pain associated with excess tension, reduces stress hormones, and increases serotonin, which provides feelings of wellbeing and enhances mental skills.

So why not make an appointment with a licensed massage therapist? If you're married, don't hesitate to treat your spouse. Research has shown that massage not only benefits the receiver but also the giver. Your husband or wife will undoubtedly want to return the favor.

He who refreshes others will himself be refreshed.

PROVERBS 11:25

IF I REALLY WANTED TO
BEAT STRESS, I WOULD . . .

MAKE TIME FOR THOSE I LOVE

WHEN IT COMES TO LOVE, "QUANTITY" TIME IS AS IMPORTANT AS QUALITY TIME.

D id you know strong relationships can help protect you from colds and the flu? When your body is stressed, hormones such as adrenaline and cortisol are increased. This lowers your immunity to the "bugs" sharing your environment. But spending time with someone you care about and who you know cares about you counteracts some of these physical changes and actually keeps you healthier.

So pick up the phone. Make a date. Take time out from your crazy schedule just to be yourself with someone you love. Plan ahead or be spontaneous. Just don't put it off. Your body will thank you and so will your heart.

Wishing to be friends is quick work, but friendship is a slow-ripening fruit.

ARISTOTLE

IF I REALLY WANTED TO
BEAT STRESS, I WOULD . . .

SPEND FIFTEEN MINUTES ORGANIZING EACH DAY

ORGANIZATION IS A DISCIPLINE NOT A PERSONALITY TRAIT.

Organizing a home, a job, and just everyday life is a monumental task. Often it's one of those projects that gets put off until you move, change jobs, or become overwhelmed by all the "stuff." But not being able to put your hands on something you need without an extensive search wastes time and increases stress.

Start small. Make a list of areas that need organization—a silverware drawer, updating an address list, filing a stack of papers, cleaning out a closet. Commit to spend fifteen minutes a day working on the areas you've listed. You'll be surprised how much you can accomplish in the first week.

Take from our souls the strain and stress, and let our ordered lives confess, the beauty of thy peace.

JOHN GREENLEAF WHITTIER

IF I REALLY WANTED TO BEAT STRESS, I WOULD . . .

BE MORE SPONTANEOUS

GETTING OFF TRACK DOESN'T HAVE TO MEAN YOUR DAY IS DERAILED.

How do you respond to the unexpected? Some personalities are just more flexible than others, but being able to "go with the flow" is an ability everyone needs to master.

Start by playing "what's the worst that could happen?" It goes like this: What would really happen if I were five minutes late or didn't clean the kitchen until the next morning? What if I played with my kids now because they asked me to rather than later as I had planned? A schedule can help you manage your time more wisely, but try writing it in pencil, instead of carving it in stone.

There is a time for everything, and a season for every activity under heaven.

ECCLESIASTES 3:1

IF I REALLY WANTED TO BEAT STRESS, I WOULD . . .

FOCUS ON ONE THING AT A TIME, AND DO IT WELL

PROPER FOCUS CAN HELP YOUR DAY DEVELOP MORE PRODUCTIVELY.

Multitasking can be a good thing. While holding on the phone, spend a few moments cleaning out that "To File" folder. While folding laundry, help your daughter review her spelling words.

But if the task at hand is more complex, doing several things at once can cause you to lose time rather than save it. Completing a complex task well takes focus. Every time you answer the phone or get a cup of coffee, it takes awhile to get back up to speed. If you need a break, take one. Relax. But when you go back to work, work. One job well done is more satisfying and less stressful than beginning six projects and leaving them all half finished.

Whatever is worth doing at all is worth doing well.

EARL OF CHESTERFIELD

If I really wanted to Beat stress, I would . . .

Shrug It Off

THE BEST TIME TO RELIEVE STRESS IS HERE AND NOW.

What you and your body really need is a massage, but here you are, stuck right in the middle of your workday. Instead of a quick trip to get a candy bar, try this exercise.

First, sit up straight in your chair. Raise your shoulders as high as you can. Hold your breath for five seconds. Then drop your shoulders and exhale through your mouth. This not only relaxes your muscles but also tricks your body into believing that you are not under a threat and do not need to take flight. So when you get stressed, shrug it off. Your body, and your boss, will appreciate it.

One day in perfect health is much.

ARABIAN PROVERB

If I really wanted to Beat stress, I would . . .

SHARE

No gift given from a sincere heart is ever too small.

"Mine, mine, mine!" It's the toddler's credo. Though not as vocal as two-year-olds, many adults hang on to what they own and what they earn just as tightly.

Sharing from a sincere heart reduces stress in two ways. First, there's the positive feeling you get from helping others, from seeing that you really can make a difference in someone else's life. Second, loosening your grip on a few things helps you hold the rest less tightly. Things happen. Prized possessions break. Financial tides turn. The less that determines who you are, the more prepared you will be to face whatever the future holds and recognize every blessing as a gift meant to be shared.

Share with God's people who are in need.

ROMANS 12:13

FIND WAYS NOT TO SPEND SO MUCH TIME IN MY CAR

STEER YOURSELF AWAY FROM DEPENDENCE ON YOUR FOUR-WHEELED FRIEND.

Traveling the back roads in a convertible may be relaxing, but commuting or carpooling through gridlock is not. Save time, money, and stress by reevaluating how often you use your car, then make a few practical changes.

Group errands. Car pool. Ride a bike. Walk. Plan days when the car stays in the garage. Look into flexible work hours where you can commute during non-peak hours. Even take a look at where you live. Consider this, if you cut just 15 minutes off of your daily commute, you will have an extra 130 hours a year. That's more than five extra days of "free time." What a stress reliever!

He who has no vision of eternity will never get a true hold of time.

THOMAS CARLYLE

IF I REALLY WANTED TO
BEAT STRESS, I WOULD . . .

APOLOGIZE

YOU WON'T BE SORRY FOR APOLOGIZING.

"I'm sorry," isn't an easy phrase to say, but it can work miracles. It's the first step toward resolving differences and relieving the stress that builds as a result of hard feelings. Admitting you were insensitive or just plain wrong is a natural lesson in humility. It may not change the way someone else feels, but when said with sincerity, it begins to change you from the inside out.

Asking for forgiveness goes a step further. It expresses more than just admitting your guilt. It voices the desire for reconciliation. Whether it's with a coworker, family member, neighbor, or even God, asking for forgiveness opens the door to healing for both your body and spirit.

Humility, like darkness, reveals the heavenly lights.

HENRY DAVID THOREAU

If I really wanted to Beat stress, I would . . .

Take God at His Word

TO TAKE GOD AT HIS WORD, YOU FIRST NEED TO KNOW WHAT HE'S SAYING.

Having someone you can trust, no matter what, is like finding a safe house in a hostile world. Even a committed spouse or well-intentioned friend may make promises they can't keep. They cannot guarantee they'll always be there or even always understand.

But God can! He's the only one who has kept every promise He's ever made. That makes Him not only faithful but trustworthy. When life is at its most stressful, relying on God's promises is a secure and relaxing respite from the storm. God has promised to be with you always, hear your prayers, forgive you, and love you unconditionally. Those are promises you can depend on.

You know with all your heart . . . That not one of all the good promises the Lord your God gave you has failed.

JOSHUA 23:14

IF I REALLY WANTED TO BEAT STRESS, I WOULD . . .

CHECK MY BLOOD PRESSURE

TRUST YOUR DOCTOR, RATHER THAN A DRUG STORE READOUT, FOR AN ACCURATE ASSESSMENT.

Stress doesn't cause high blood pressure. However, having a "stress-prone" personality can be a risk factor, along with heredity, a sedentary lifestyle, being overweight, and excessive salt or alcohol consumption.

Hypertension means your heart is working harder than it should to pump blood through your body. It increases your risk of stroke, heart disease, and kidney failure. Having two or more blood pressure readings greater than 140/99 means it's time to take action. Exercise, diet, weight reduction, relaxation techniques, and possibly medication can help. But first you need to be aware of the problem. Checking your blood pressure takes just a few moments of your time, but it can add years to your life.

Look to your health; and if you have it, praise God.

IZAAK WALTON

If I really wanted to Beat stress, I would . . .

Give my Answering Machine a Workout

TO PICK UP . . . OR NOT TO PICK UP, THAT IS THE QUESTION.

Home phone. Work phone. Cell phone. Some people can be reached anywhere at any time. Though it may be convenient, it can also be a time-wasting interruption and a source of stress.

Getting caller ID to screen unwanted calls is a small step toward independence. Then let your answering machine do its job on a more regular basis. Don't answer the phone during dinner or "family times." Schedule a morning or two a week at work where its common knowledge others should "leave a message." Schedule time in the afternoon, when your energy is not as high, to return calls. Don't ignore those who call, just fit them into a more productive, less interruptive schedule.

So much they talk'd, so very little said.

CHARLES CHURCHILL

STARE AT A STAR

LIFE IS A GIFT TO BE CELEBRATED NOT A TASK TO BE TACKLED.

Life is bigger than your "to do" list. But it's easy to lose perspective when your days are spent running from one appointment to the next, putting out one fire after another, and always feeling as though you're lagging just a bit behind the Joneses.

Stop—even if just for a moment. Take a good look at the world around you, meditating on the mystery of a distant star, the brilliance of a fleeting sunset, the miracle of there being only one you throughout all of eternity. It is liberating to ponder being such a tiny speck in a seemingly limitless universe and yet so deeply loved by such a great God.

He determines the number of the stars and calls them each by name.

PSALM 147:4

If I really wanted to Beat stress, I would . . .

Rearrange my Work Area

MAKE A DATE TO REDECORATE!

Though your work area may feel like a natural stress magnet, a few changes can actually help relieve tension. Throw out or file the piles. Add a poster, toy, or photo that makes you smile. Something downright silly may actually brighten someone else's day, as well as your own.

If you're staring at a computer screen all day, give your eyes a break. You can relieve eyestrain by moving your eyes to something in the distance every thirty minutes or so. A poster with a horizon line is especially soothing. That's because your eyes are at rest when they look at infinity. Also, adding a decorative element in a vibrant shade of red will have an energy-boosting effect on your body.

The reward of one duty is the power to fulfill another.

GEORGE ELIOT

IF I REALLY WANTED TO BEAT STRESS, I WOULD . . .

SPEAK UP

A QUIET PERSON IS NOT SYNONYMOUS WITH A CALM PERSON.

Not everyone is an extrovert—but everyone's opinion counts. If you feel you are often being taken advantage of, ignored, or discounted, and you hold your feelings inside, your body is bottling up your "fight-or-flight" response. This can produce rapid, shallow breathing, a quickening of your pulse, and an increase in your blood pressure. Your body is speaking volumes, even if your mouth isn't.

If standing up for yourself doesn't come naturally to you, try it in small doses. Write down how you feel. Pray about it. Then set up a time to talk with the person in question. Postpone a confrontation until you are calm and thinking clearly. But don't just forget it. Your body won't.

It is better to debate a question without settling it than to settle a question without debating it.

JOSEPH JOUBERT

IF I REALLY WANTED TO
BEAT STRESS, I WOULD . . .

ASK FOR A HUG

SOMETIMES, ENCOURAGEMENT DOESN'T REQUIRE WORDS.

A pat on your shoulder. The brush of a caring hand. A warm embrace. Your body considers them all a momentary massage. A friendly touch is a trigger for your body to release stress-relieving chemicals that help calm you down. Better yet, it helps you feel more connected to others, more deeply cared for and loved.

Not everyone is a "hugger." Learning to read others' body language and know when touch is welcome and when to draw the line takes time and sensitivity. But being able to give and receive a hug is a skill worth acquiring and a comfort worth savoring.

To everything there is a season . . . a time to embrace, and a time to refrain from embracing.

ECCLESIASTES 3:1,5 NKJV

If I really wanted to Beat stress, I would . . .

Clean out my Inbox

Why not file instead of pile?

How long has it been since you've seen the bottom of your inbox? For many people, it's the closest thing to a black hole they'll ever find here on earth. Unfortunately, what's "hottest" keeps taking precedence and whatever can be put off until later sinks to the bottom, not to be seen again until you relocate.

Making a commitment to rediscover the bottom of your inbox at least once a month is a great way to gain better control over your workload, which can reduce feelings of stress. Monitoring what goes into your inbox is the first step. Try to handle paper only once. File it, deal with it, or toss it.

Our main business is not to see what lies dimly at a distance, but to do what lies clearly at hand.

Thomas Carlyle

IF I REALLY WANTED TO
BEAT STRESS, I WOULD . . .

TURN OFF THE TUBE

DON'T MISS YOUR OWN REAL-LIFE DRAMA.

Watching television looks like a relaxing activity, and relaxation means stress reducing, right? Not necessarily. Research has shown that people usually feel worse after spending time watching TV, not better.

Television's main benefit is diversion. There's nothing wrong with a little diversion now and then, but when turning on the TV is as automatic as eating dinner every night, it can become a means of procrastination instead of relaxation. It replaces chores that need to be done, bills that need to be paid, and relationships that could use a little personal time. Tonight, why not put down the remote and give your brain a workout with a good book. Or just sit back and watch the sunset. It's never a rerun.

What goes into the mind comes out in a life.

CHRISTIAN BOOKSELLERS ASSOCIATION

IF I REALLY WANTED TO BEAT STRESS, I WOULD . . .

DOWNSIZE MY LIFE

THINK SMALL.

Bigger is better, at least according to American advertising. But "bigger" takes more work to maintain. A larger house takes more time to clean. A larger car takes more gasoline, which costs more money, which takes more of your workday to earn. A larger "life," filled to the brim with possessions and commitments, takes a much larger slice of your time and energy. How much are you willing to exchange for "bigger"?

And remember, one of the best anti-stress measures begins with downsizing your agenda. Try to schedule only 75 percent of your time instead of 110 percent. You'll find that dropping some activities makes it possible to receive greater enjoyment from the others. Sometimes, less really is more!

A plain and simple life is a full life.

PROVERBS 13:7 MSG

If I really wanted to Beat stress, I would . . .

Laugh, Giggle, Chortle, and Snort

TAKE LIFE SERIOUSLY AND YOURSELF LIGHTLY.

To your body, laughter is exercise. Your blood pressure and heart rate rise briefly, then drop below their original levels, just like at the gym. Laughter even increases white blood cells, which fight disease.

So go ahead and laugh. Rent a funny movie. Trade jokes with a friend. Go to a stationery store and read the greeting cards. Send a few of your favorites as surprise stress relievers to friends. Decorate your home and office with things that make you smile—posters with humorous sayings, wacky art, tacky souvenirs. Try to find the humor in stressful situations. Don't hold it in. Learn the art of the guffaw. It's good for you.

It is the heart that is not yet sure of its God that is afraid to laugh in His presence.

GEORGE MACDONALD

IF I REALLY WANTED TO
BEAT STRESS, I WOULD . . .

CRY MY HEART OUT

A TEAR CAN ONLY BE DRIED ONCE IT'S BEEN CRIED.

The shortest verse in the Bible is, "Jesus wept" (John 11:35). Jesus' tears were over the death of a friend—someone whom Jesus knew He would momentarily raise from the dead. But still, He wept.

There are things in this life worth crying over. Even God acknowledges that. Psalm 56:8 says that God keeps every one of your tears in a bottle. How big is that bottle? Is it a gallon jug or vial so small it holds hardly a trace of salt? Whatever tears are not released from the eyes are stored in the heart. And a heavy heart can be a silent, constant stressor. So give yourself permission to let down and let go. God's shoulder is always available.

Tears are often the telescope by which men see far into heaven.

HENRY WARD BEECHER

IF I REALLY WANTED TO BEAT STRESS, I WOULD . . .

CHOOSE LIFE

Not choosing is still making a choice.

Every day is a deluge of choices. And every decision, no matter how small, is accompanied by some stress. But there's one decision you need to make every day that will actually lower your anxiety levels—choosing life.

Choosing life is more than just choosing to keep eating and breathing. It's choosing to make the most of where you are, what you have, what you're doing, and who you're with. It's choosing to look at life optimistically. That doesn't mean closing your eyes to life's problems, just recognizing they will come to an end. It's been shown that optimists have fewer medical problems than pessimists. What's more important is how much more joy they get out of life.

I have set before you life and death, blessings and curses. Now choose life.

DEUTERONOMY 30:19

IF I REALLY WANTED TO BEAT STRESS, I WOULD . . .

LISTEN TO MUSIC

THE RIGHT BEAT CAN HELP YOU BEAT STRESS.

Though singing and dancing have their own anti-stress benefits, just listening to music also does wonderful things for your body. If you're looking for instant relaxation, choose music with a rhythm slower than your natural heart rate—about seventy-two beats a minute. Classical or mellow jazz with a repetitive musical pattern is especially calming. If you need a boost of energy, go for rock and roll or something with a Latin beat.

What's most important is finding music that moves you according to your own personal taste. Taking a moment to close your eyes and listen, without doing anything else, is an instant pick-me-up. For even more stress- busting benefits, put on some headphones and take a walk around the block.

Music expresses that which cannot be said and on which it is impossible to keep silent.

VICTOR HUGO

If I really wanted to Beat stress, I would . . .

Limit my Time with High-Need People

Stress is often contagious.

S pending time with a good friend can actually lower your blood pressure. But what do you do with people who seem to raise it? Some you can choose not to deal with, but with others, particularly family members or coworkers, the solution may be more difficult.

Prepare for those inevitable encounters with the high-need people in your life by first dealing with any unresolved conflict. Next, reprogram yourself not to go into overdrive every time you see them. Let their presence become a trigger to breathe more deeply and consciously relax your body. Pray. Get caller ID and choose when you're going to speak to them. And always give yourself an out by scheduling other appointments around time planned with them.

Search thy own heart; what paineth thee in others in thyself may be.

John Greenleaf Whittier

If I really wanted to
Beat stress, I would . . .

Contemplate Heaven

WHEN LIFE GETS YOU DOWN, DON'T FORGET TO LOOK UP.

Some days, you catch a glimpse of Heaven. Perhaps it's the birth of your first child or watching a sunset reflecting on ocean waves. At those times, your heart may whisper, "This is as good as it gets." But most days your heart says exactly the opposite, "There's got to be more to life!"

What your heart's really saying is, "There's no place like home." God created us to live a life with Him where there's no more death, tears, mortgage, deadlines, or stress. And God's character suggests that Heaven will be much more like a lively wedding feast than an endless choir rehearsal. Now that's something to look forward to!

He puts a little of heaven in our hearts so that we'll never settle for less.

2 CORINTHIANS 5:5 MSG

IF I REALLY WANTED TO BEAT STRESS, I WOULD . . .

LOVE EXTRAVAGANTLY

DON'T JUST LEND A HAND, GIVE YOUR HEART.

There's one sure way to kill love—measure it. Loving someone because you think it's the right thing to do, because it's "your turn," or simply for what you can get isn't love at all. It's manipulation.

Keeping records of any kind can be a stressful job, but with love, it can be deadly— especially to a relationship. If it's true that the more love you give away, the more you have, do yourself a favor and love those who aren't in a position to return it. Give in secret. Volunteer. Pamper your spouse or a friend without expectations of the favor being returned. It's a stress reliever that has benefits not only for you but also for everyone around you.

To ease another's heartache is to forget one's own.

ABRAHAM LINCOLN

IF I REALLY WANTED TO
BEAT STRESS, I WOULD . . .

KEEP A JOURNAL

WRITING IS A RELEASE FOR YOUR BODY AND SOUL.

A journal is like a friend who's always available and will never judge you. In it, you can write down your darkest secrets, most irrational fears, persistent worries, and craziest ideas, without the fear of being rejected, laughed at, or graded.

Bottling up strong emotions builds up stress. Releasing these emotions through writing aids your immune system and improves your overall physical health. It can also help you analyze and sort out problems instead of just stewing over them. Try writing for twenty minutes several times a week. Don't grade yourself on spelling or creativity. Just write. After a few weeks, write about how journaling has made you feel. Research suggests you'll be pleasantly surprised.

Look within.

MARCUS AURELIUS

If I REALLY WANTED TO
BEAT STRESS, I WOULD . . .

SCHEDULE A REGULAR CHECKUP

FINDING A DOCTOR YOU CAN TALK
TO IS THE FIRST STEP TOWARD A
HEALTHIER YOU.

Not all physical ailments send up a red flag. Some show up with a quiet whisper. Exhaustion. Trouble sleeping. Headaches. Indigestion. Difficulty concentrating. Depression. Though all of these may be symptoms of stress run amok, they may also be signs of more serious medical problems.

An annual checkup, resulting in an informed diagnosis, is extra insurance in your fight against stress. It helps you make sure that stress is actually what you're fighting. Your doctor can also give you some up-to-date tips on dealing with stress and relieve you of any worries you may be holding on to about ongoing aches and pains.

Dear friend, I pray that you may enjoy good
health and that all may go well with you.

3 JOHN 2

If I really wanted to Beat stress, I would . . .

Have a Chat with my Heavenly Father

GETTING ON YOUR KNEES HELPS
YOU GET BACK UP ON YOUR FEET.

A car is driving on the wrong side of the road, headed straight for you. What's your first thought? In life-or-death situations, it's often that little voice that yells out, "Oh, God, no!" or "Please, help me!" Everyone knows how to pray. It's a natural part of life, but too often it's reserved for those moments when you know without a doubt that circumstances are out of your hands.

Talking over problems with a friend has been shown to reduce stress. And God is a good and faithful friend—one who actually has the power to help. Share the details of your life with Him. He cares.

Certain thoughts are prayers. There are moments when, whatever the attitude of the body, the soul is on its knees.

VICTOR HUGO

If I really wanted to beat stress, I would . . .

Let God Be God

THE KEY TO SUCCESS, WITHOUT EXTRA STRESS, IS LETTING GOD DO HIS JOB.

Being God is quite an endeavor. All powerful. All knowing. Able to be everywhere at once. Holy. Just. Infallible. The essence of love itself. We human beings don't measure up, but that doesn't seem to keep us from trying. Sound familiar? If so, it may be time to practice the art of letting God be God.

As you have probably already discovered, feeling ultimately responsible for your own life and the lives of others can be incredibly stressful—and futile. None of us really have much to say about what life brings our way. So tackle the biggest step toward beating stress— make good, informed choices, plan and prepare, work hard, and leave the rest to God.

Pile your troubles on God's shoulders he'll carry your load, he'll help you out.

PSALM 55:22 MSG